WEEKLY WR READER®
EARLY LEARNING LIBRARY

LET'S READ
ABOUT
Animals
CONOZCAMOS
A LOS
animales

Kangaroos/
Canguros

by/por Kathleen Pohl

Reading consultant/Consultora de lectura:
Susan Nations, M.Ed.,
author, literacy coach, consultant in literacy
development/autora, tutora de alfabetización,
consultora de desarrollo de la lectura

Please visit our web site at: www.garethstevens.com
For a free color catalog describing Weekly Reader® Early Learning Library's list
of high-quality books, call 1-877-445-5824 (USA) or 1-800-387-3178 (Canada).
Weekly Reader® Early Learning Library's fax: (414) 336-0164.

Library of Congress Cataloging-in-Publication Data

Pohl, Kathleen.
  [Kangaroos. Spanish and English]
  Kangaroos = Canguros / by/por Kathleen Pohl.
    p. cm. — (Let's read about animals = Conozcamos a los animales)
  Includes bibliographical references and index.
  ISBN-13: 978-0-8368-8006-9 (lib. bdg.)
  ISBN-13: 978-0-8368-8013-7 (softcover)
  1. Kangaroos—Juvenile literature. I. Title. II. Title: Canguros.
  QL737.M35P6418   2007
  599.2'22—dc22   2006037434

This edition first published in 2007 by
Weekly Reader® Early Learning Library
A Member of the WRC Media Family of Companies
330 West Olive Street, Suite 100
Milwaukee, WI 53212 USA

Editor: Dorothy L. Gibbs
Art Direction: Tammy West
Cover design and page layout: Kami Strunsee
Picture research: Diane Laska-Swanke
Spanish translation: Tatiana Acosta and Guillermo Gutiérrez

Picture credits: Cover, title © Ferrero-Labat/Auscape; pp. 5, 7, 15, 19 © Jean-Paul Ferrero/Auscape;
p. 9 Kami Strunsee/© Weekly Reader® Early Learning Library; p. 11 © Graham Robertson/Auscape;
p. 13 © Owen Newman/naturepl.com; pp. 17, 21 © John Cancalosi/Auscape

Printed in the United States of America

1 2 3 4 5 6 7 8 9 10 10 09 08 07 06

Note to Educators and Parents

Reading is such an exciting adventure for young children! They are beginning to integrate their oral language skills with written language. To encourage children along the path to early literacy, books must be colorful, engaging, and interesting; they should invite the young reader to explore both the print and the pictures.

The *Let's Read About Animals* series is designed to help children read and learn about the special characteristics and behaviors of the intriguing featured animals. Each book is an informative nonfiction companion to one of the colorful and charming fiction books in the *Animal Storybooks* series.

Each book in the *Let's Read About Animals* series is specially designed to support the young reader in the reading process. The familiar topics are appealing to young children and invite them to read — and reread — again and again. The full-color photographs and enhanced text further support the student during the reading process.

In addition to serving as wonderful picture books in schools, libraries, homes, and other places where children learn to love reading, these books are specifically intended to be read within an instructional guided reading group. This small group setting allows beginning readers to work with a fluent adult model as they make meaning from the text. After children develop fluency with the text and content, the books can be read independently. Children and adults alike will find these books supportive, engaging, and fun!

— Susan Nations, M.Ed., author/literacy coach/
consultant in literacy development

Nota para los maestros y los padres

¡Leer es una aventura tan emocionante para los niños pequeños! A esta edad están comenzando a integrar su manejo del lenguaje oral con el lenguaje escrito. Para animar a los niños en el camino de la lectura incipiente, los libros deben ser coloridos, estimulantes e interesantes; deben invitar a los jóvenes lectores a explorar la letra impresa y las ilustraciones.

Conozcamos a los animales es una nueva colección diseñada para que los niños conozcan las características y comportamientos de los interesantes animales que se presentan. Cada libro es un texto informativo de no ficción que acompaña a uno de los libros de ficción en lengua inglesa de la colección *Animal Storybooks*.

Cada libro de la serie *Conozcamos a los animales* está especialmente diseñado para ayudar a los jóvenes lectores en el proceso de lectura. Los temas familiares llaman la atención de los niños y los invitan a leer una y otra vez. Las fotografías a todo color y el tamaño de la letra ayudan aún más al estudiante en el proceso de lectura.

Además de servir como maravillosos libros ilustrados en escuelas, bibliotecas, hogares y otros lugares donde los niños aprenden a amar la lectura, estos libros han sido especialmente concebidos para ser leídos en un grupo de lectura guiada. Este contexto permite que los lectores incipientes trabajen con un adulto que domina la lectura mientras van determinando el significado del texto. Una vez que los niños dominan el texto y el contenido, el libro puede ser leído de manera independiente. ¡Estos libros les resultarán útiles, estimulantes y divertidos a niños y a adultos por igual!

— Susan Nations, M.Ed., autora/tutora de alfabetización/
consultora de desarrollo de la lectura

You might see a **kangaroo** at a zoo. Look for a furry animal that has big back feet and hops!

Si quieres ver un **canguro**, puedes ir a un zoológico. ¡Busca a un animal peludo, con grandes patas traseras y que brinca!

Kangaroos can hop very fast.
Sometimes, they look like they
are flying!

Los canguros pueden brincar muy
deprisa. A veces, ¡parece como
si volaran!

There are many kinds of kangaroos. They all come from **Australia** (aw-STRAY-lee-ah). The map shows where red kangaroos and gray kangaroos live in the wild.

Hay muchos tipos de canguros. Todos vienen de **Australia**. El mapa muestra dónde viven en estado salvaje los canguros rojos y los canguros grises.

Australia/Australia

Tasmania/
Tasmania

Map Key/Clave del mapa

places red kangaroos live/lugares
donde viven los canguros rojos

places gray kangaroos live/lugares
donde viven los canguros grises

places red and gray kangaroos live/
lugares donde viven los canguros
rojos y los canguros grises

9

Some kangaroos are very small. Others
may be very tall. Red kangaroos are
the biggest of all!

Algunos canguros son muy pequeños.
Otros pueden ser muy altos. ¡Los
canguros rojos son los más grandes!

red kangaroos/
canguros rojos

1

Sometimes, kangaroos fight. They look like they are boxing!

Algunas veces, los canguros luchan. ¡Parece que están boxeando!

Kangaroos live in groups called **mobs**. They rest most of the day. It is too hot to move around!

Los canguros viven en grupos llamados **manadas**. Pasan la mayor parte del día descansando. ¡Hace demasiado calor para moverse!

At night, kangaroos move around a lot. They like to eat at night. Kangaroos eat grass and leaves.

Durante la noche, los canguros se desplazan mucho. Les gusta comer de noche. Los canguros comen hierba y hojas.

The body of a newborn kangaroo has a shape like a jelly bean. The baby is called a **joey** (joh-ee).

El cuerpo de un canguro recién nacido tiene forma de frijol pequeño. En Australia, una cría de canguro recibe el nombre de *joey*.

newborn joey/
canguro recién nacido

A joey grows inside its mother's **pouch** for many months. Then, it peeks out. Welcome to the world, little joey!

Una cría de canguro crece dentro del **marsupio** de su madre durante muchos meses. Después, saca la cabeza. ¡Bienvenido al mundo, cangurito!

joey/
cría de canguro

pouch/
marsupio

Glossary/Glosario

Australia — an island continent in the southern half of the world

joey — a baby animal that grows in its mother's pouch, such as a kangaroo or a koala

mobs — groups of kangaroos

pouch — the special pocket that kangaroos and some other animals have on their bellies and use to hold their babies

---

Australia — isla continente en la mitad sur del mundo

joey — nombre que se da en Australia a la cría de animal que crece en el marsupio de su madre, como la de canguro o la de koala

manadas — grupos de canguros

marsupio — bolsa que tienen en el vientre los canguros y otros animales para llevar a las crías

For More Information/Más información

Books

Jumping Kangaroos. Pull Ahead Books (series).
Michelle Levine (Lerner Publications)

The Kangaroo. Life Cycles (series). Diana Noonan
(Chelsea Clubhouse)

A Kangaroo Joey Grows Up. Baby Animals (series).
Joan Hewett (Carolrhoda Books)

The Kangaroos' Great Escape. Animal Storybooks (series).
Rebecca Johnson (Gareth Stevens)

Libros

El canguro. Lee y aprende: Animales del zoológico (series).
Patricia Whitehouse (Heinemann Library)

Los pantaloncillos de canguro. Realidad y ficción: Cuentos
de animales (series). Anders Hanson (SandCastle)

Index/Índice

About the Author/Información sobre la autora

Kathleen Pohl has written and edited many children's books. Among them are animal tales, rhyming books, retold classics, and the forty-book series *Nature Close-Ups*. She and her husband, Bruce, live in the middle of beautiful Wisconsin woods and share their home with six goats, a llama, and all kinds of wonderful woodland creatures.

Kathleen Pohl ha escrito y corregido muchos libros infantiles. Entre ellos hay cuentos de animales, libros de rimas, versiones nuevas de cuentos clásicos y la serie de cuarenta libros *Nature Close-Ups*. Kathleen vive con su marido, Bruce, en medio de los bellos bosques de Wisconsin. Ambos comparten su hogar con seis cabras, una llama y todo tipo de maravillosos animales del bosque.